The Beauty of Motherhood

The Beauty of Motherhood

SELECTED WRITINGS ABOUT
THE JOYS OF BEING A MOTHER

Edited by Bette Bishop

Color Illustrations by Frieda D. Senn

HALLMARK EDITIONS

*A complete list of acknowledgments
appears at the end of this book.*

The Beauty of Motherhood

When God thought of mother,
He must have laughed with satisfaction,
and framed it quickly—
so rich, so deep, so divine,
so full of soul, power, and beauty,
was the conception.

HENRY WARD BEECHER

A Mother's Picture

A lady, the loveliest ever the sun looked
  down upon,
You must paint for me.
O, if I could only make you see
The clear blue eyes, the tender smile,
The sovereign sweetness, the gentle grace,
The woman's soul, and the angel's face,
That are beaming on me all the while,
But I need not speak these foolish words;
  One word tells you all I would say,
She is my mother; and you will agree
  That all the rest may be thrown away.

ALICE CARY

6

Story of my Life

I cannot recall what happened during the first months after my illness. I only know that I sat in my mother's lap or clung to her dress as she went about her household duties. My hands felt every object and observed every motion, and in this way I learned to know many things. Soon I felt the need of some communication with others and began to make crude signs. A shake of the head meant "No" and a nod, "Yes," a pull meant "Come" and a push, "Go." Was it bread that I wanted? Then I would imitate the acts of cutting the slices and buttering them. If I wanted my mother to make ice cream for dinner I made the sign for working the freezer and shivered, indicating cold. My mother, moreover, succeeded in making me understand a good deal. I always knew when she wished me to bring her something, and I would run upstairs or anywhere else she indicated. Indeed, I owe to her loving wisdom all that was bright and good in my long night.

HELEN KELLER

What Is a Home?

A roof to keep out the rain. Four walls to
keep out the wind. Floors to keep out the
cold. Yes, but home is more than that. It
is the laugh of a baby, the song of a mother,
the strength of a father. Warmth of loving
hearts, light from happy eyes, kindness,
loyalty, comradeship. Home is first school
and first church for young ones, where they
learn what is right, what is good, and what
is kind. Where they go for comfort when
they are hurt or sick. Where joy is shared
and sorrow eased. Where fathers and mothers
are respected and loved. Where children
are wanted. Where the simplest food is good
enough for kings because it is earned.
Where money is not so important as loving-
kindness. Where even the teakettle sings
from happiness. That is home. God bless it.

ERNESTINE SCHUMAN-HEINK

Sharing With God

Every mother has the breathtaking privilege
of sharing with God in the creation of new
life. She helps bring into existence a
soul that will endure for all eternity.

Every mother also has the unique honor of
nurturing and developing the bit of divine
greatness in her child. Through her loving
and devoted care, this youthful power can be
directed from its earliest years to work for
the glory of God and the benefit of others
and thus contribute to its own temporal and
eternal advantage.

Yes, a good mother can reach beyond the
sanctuary of her home and help renew the
face of the earth.

JAMES KELLER

9

"Say Hello to Grandma"

Across the miles a tiny "Hi" —
I strain my ears to hear.
"How are you darling?" "Fine," he says.
I dab away a tear.
Three costly minutes — two small words —
But who can count their worth?
They've proved beyond a doubt that he's
The smartest child on earth!
Three costly minutes — two small words —
A waste of money? Maybe —
But then you're not the Grandma
Of the world's most brilliant baby!

HELEN LOWRIE MARSHALL

What Is a Mother?

A mother can be almost any size or any age, but she won't admit to anything over thirty. A mother has soft hands and smells good. A mother likes new dresses, music, a clean house, her children's kisses, an automatic washer and Daddy.

A mother doesn't like having her children sick, muddy feet, temper tantrums, loud noise or bad report cards. A mother can read a thermometer (much to the amazement of Daddy) and like magic, can kiss a hurt away.

A mother can bake good cakes and pies but likes to see her children eat vegetables. A mother can stuff a fat baby into a snow suit in seconds and can kiss sad little faces and make them smile.

A mother is underpaid, has long hours and gets very little rest. She worries too much about her children but she says she doesn't mind at all. And no matter how old her children are, she still likes to think of them as her little babies.

She is the guardian angel of the family, the queen, the tender hand of love. A mother is the best friend anyone ever has. A mother is love.

AUTHOR UNKNOWN

The Princess

I loved her, one
Not learned, save in gracious household ways,
Nor perfect, nay, but full of tender wants,
No Angel, but a dearer being, all dipt
In Angel instincts, breathing Paradise,
Interpreter between the gods and men,
Who look'd all native to her place, and yet
On tiptoe seem'd to touch upon a sphere
Too gross to tread,
    and all male minds perforce
Sway'd to her from their orbits
    as they moved,
And girdled her with music. Happy he
With such a mother! faith in womenkind
Beats with his blood,
    and trust in all things high
Comes easy to him, and tho' he trip and fall,
He shall not blind his soul with clay.

ALFRED, LORD TENNYSON

Only One Mother

Hundreds of stars in the pretty sky,
  Hundreds of shells on the shore together,
Hundreds of birds that go singing by,
  Hundreds of birds in the sunny weather.

Hundreds of dewdrops to greet the dawn,
  Hundreds of bees in the purple clover,
Hundreds of butterflies on the lawn,
  But only one mother the wide world over.

AUTHOR UNKNOWN

Why God Made Mothers

God knew that everybody needs
Someone to show the way,
He knew that babies need someone
To care for them each day . . .
He knew they needed someone sweet
To soothe their baby cries,
To teach them how to walk and talk,
And sing them lullabies . . .
That's why God made mothers.

He knew small children need someone
To lend a guiding hand,
To answer all their questions
And to smile and understand,
Someone to read them storybooks,
To teach them wrong from right,
To show them wonderful new games,
And hear their prayers at night . . .
That's why God made mothers.

And then throughout their childhood years,
God knew that children need
Someone to smile at them with pride,
Encourage each new deed.
As they grow up and all their lives,
God knew that everywhere,
All children need a mother's heart
To understand and care,
And that's why God made mothers.

KATHERINE NELSON DAVIS

What Is a Mother?

What is a mother? Who shall answer this?
A mother is a font and spring of life,
A mother is a forest in whose heart
Lies hid a secret ancient as the hills,
For men to claim and take its wealth away;
And like the forest shall her wealth renew
And give, and give again, that men may live.

FRANCIS CARDINAL SPELLMAN

The Teacher

Into the woman's keeping is committed the destiny of the generations to come after us. In bringing up your children you mothers must remember that while it is essential to be loving and tender it is no less essential to be wise and firm. Foolishness and affection must not be treated as interchangeable terms; and besides training your sons and daughters in the softer and milder virtues, you must seek to give them those stern and hardy qualities which in after life they will surely need.

Some children will go wrong in spite of the best training; and some will go right even when their surroundings are most unfortunate.... Teach boys and girls alike that they are not to look forward to lives spent in avoiding difficulties; teach them that work, for themselves and also for others, is not a curse but a blessing; seek to make them happy, to make them enjoy life, but seek also to make them face life with steadfast resolution, and to do their whole duty before God and to man. Surely she who can thus train her sons and daughters is thrice fortunate among women.

THEODORE ROOSEVELT

A Cradle Hymn

Hush! my dear, lie still and slumber,
  Holy angels guard thy bed!
Heavenly blessings without number
  Gently falling on thy head.

Sleep, my babe; thy food and raiment,
  House and home, thy friends provide;
All without thy care or payment:
  All thy wants are well supplied.

ISAAC WATTS

Home

This is the true nature of home—it is the place of Peace; the shelter, not only from all injury, but from all terror, doubt and division. In so far as it is not this, it is not home....

But so far as it is a sacred place, a vestal temple, a temple of the hearth watched over by Household Gods, before whose faces none may come but those whom they can receive with love,—so far as it is this, and roof and fire are types only of a nobler shade and light,—shade as of the rock in a weary land, and light as of the Pharos in the stormy sea,—so far it vindicates the name, and fulfills the praise, of home.

And wherever a true wife comes, this home is always round her. The stars only may be over her head; the glowworm in the night—cold grass may be the only fire at her foot; but home is yet wherever she is; and for a noble woman it stretches far round her, better than ceiled with cedar, or painted with vermilion, shedding its quiet light far, for those who else were homeless.

JOHN RUSKIN

Mother's Hands

I remember she used often to look somewhat ruefully at her hands, those beautiful, useful, roughened hands of hers, so strong in the palm, so unexpectedly delicate and pointed in the fingers; not small hands, but having spare and well-shaped lines. It was always her plan that one day she would stop plunging her hands into this and that; she was going to wear gloves when she gardened and use cold cream and have really "nice" hands. She loved the white hands of ladies, the skin soft and smooth and the nails pink and tapering. But if she ever remembered to put on gloves, as sometimes once in a long time she did, sooner or later they would be off and she would be grubbing about in the earth, looking up to say apologetically, "I seem to have to feel the roots are right. They won't grow otherwise. And I do like the feel of the earth!"

PEARL BUCK

A Mother's Love

There is not a grand inspiring thought,
There is not a truth by wisdom taught,
There is not a feeling pure and high,
That may not be read in a mother's eye.

There are teachings in earth and sky and air,
The heavens the glory of God declare;
But louder than voice, beneath, above,
He is heard to speak through a mother's love.

EMILY TAYLOR

Her World

Number four (the ten-o'clock passenger) wheezed tardily, like an asthmatic old man, up to the station, and pulled out as soon as three people had alighted in the dark and the rain.... One third of the incoming passengers this drizzling night was Mrs. Edward Everett Cutter.

...Ed Cutter, big and solid and substantial-looking, stood under the eaves of the dripping station holding an umbrella and a flashlight, like the masculine version of the Goddess of Liberty. He grinned a whole-hearted, cheerful welcome at the sight of his trim-looking wife. Many a woman has been met at a pier after a transatlantic voyage with less sincere gratitude for her return.

... They were on the last block now and the light shone in the windows of home. Nell hastened her steps unconsciously. That low, rambling house set well back in the big yard was her world. ... There are people who say the lives of such women are narrow. They are not narrow. They are as wide as sympathy and as broad as love. ... A person may encircle the globe with mind open only to bodily comfort. Another may live his life on a sixty-foot lot and listen to the voices of the universe.

BESS STREETER ALDRICH

She Shall be Praised

Who can find a virtuous woman? for her price is far above rubies.

Strength and honour are her clothing; and she shall rejoice in time to come.

She openeth her mouth with wisdom; and in her tongue is the law of kindness.

She looketh well to the ways of her household, and eateth not the bread of idleness.

Her children arise up, and call her blessed; her husband also, and he praiseth her.

Many daughters have done virtuously, but thou excellest them all.

Favour is deceitful, and beauty is vain: but a woman that feareth the Lord, she shall be praised.

Give her the fruit of her hands; and let her own works praise her in the gates.

PROVERBS 31: 10, 25-31

The Palace and the Hut

Part One: As night fell and the lights glittered in the great house . . . the nobles entered, dressed in gorgeous raiment. . . . The instruments filled the air with pleasant melodies while the dignitaries danced to the soothing music.

At midnight the finest and most palatable foods were served on a beautiful table. . . . The feasters dined and drank abundantly, until the sequence of the wine began to play its part. At dawn the throng dispersed boisterously, after spending a long night of intoxication and gluttony which hurried their worn bodies into their deep beds with unnatural sleep.

Part Two: At eventide, a man attired in the dress of heavy work stood before the door of his small house . . . he entered and greeted the occupants in a cheerful manner, and then sat between his children who were playing at the fireplace. In a

short time, his wife had the meal prepared and they sat at a wooden table consuming their food. After eating they gathered around the oil lamp and talked of the day's events. When early night had lapsed, all stood silently and surrendered themselves to the King of Slumber with a song of praise and a prayer of gratitude upon their lips.

KAHLIL GIBRAN

Motherhood

Womanliness means only motherhood;
All love begins and ends there, — roams
  enough,
But, having run the circle, rests at home.

ROBERT BROWNING

Woman Deeply Loved

To see and watch her is to know
That she is deeply loved. Her face
Reflects this. Love has left its trace
In her serenity, the glow
Of deep contentment in her eyes,
Her joyous laugh, the cheerful way
She goes about her work each day.
Love haloes women, beautifies
The plainest face, for more than bread
To every woman is the knowing
She is cherished; keeps her glowing
With confidence, affection-fed:
Her happiness so much a part
Of love, enshrined within her heart.

VELMA WEST SYKES

28

To My Mother

They tell us of an Indian tree
  Which howsoe'er the sun and sky
May tempt its boughs to wander free,
  And shoot and blossom, wide and high,
Downward again to that dear earth
  From which the life that fills and warms
Its grateful being, first had birth.
  'Tis thus, though wooed by flattering
                         friends,
And fed with fame (if fame it may be),
  This heart, my own dear mother, bends,
With love's true instance, back to thee!

THOMAS MOORE

Mother

... The angels, whispering to one another,
Can find, among their burning terms of love,
None so devotional as that of "Mother"....

EDGAR ALLAN POE

29

The Heroism of the Mother

Is not the highest heroism that which is free even from the approbation of the best and wisest? The heroism which is known only to our Father, who seeth in secret? The God-like lives lived in obscurity? How many thousands of heroines there must be now, of whom we shall never know. But still they are there. They sow in secret the seed of which we pluck the flower, and eat the fruit, and know not that we pass the sower daily in the streets.

One form of heroism — the most common, and yet the least remembered of all — namely, the heroism of the average mother. Ah! When I think of that broad fact, I gather hope again for poor humanity; and this dark world looks bright — this diseased world looks wholesome to me once more — because, whatever else it is not full of, it is at least full of mothers.

CHARLES KINGSLEY

The Picture

The painter has with his brush transferred
the landscape to the canvas with such fidelity
that the trees and grasses seem almost
real; he has made even the face of a maiden
seem instinct with life, but there is one
picture so beautiful that no painter has ever
been able perfectly to reproduce it, and that
is the picture of the mother holding in her
arms her babe.

WILLIAM JENNINGS BRYAN

Mother

I think it was a girlish hand,
  Unlined, well tended, when it held
At first, my clinging baby hand
  In gentle grasp by love impelled.

I think it was a youthful face
  That bent above me as I lay
Asleep, and bright the eyes that watched
  My rest, in that forgotten day.

I think it was a slender form
  That bore my weight on tiring arm,
And swift young feet that watched my steps
  To guide them from the ways of harm.

But years and cares have changed that form
  And face and hand; have streaked with gray
The hair; yet is the heart as full
  Of love as in that other day.

And she has her reward; not fame,
  Or baubles bought in any mart,
But motherhood's brave crown, the love
  And homage of her own child's heart.

CLARA AIKEN SPEER

Because She Is A Mother

She broke the bread into two fragments, and gave them to the children, who ate with avidity. "She hath kept none for herself," grumbled the Sergeant. "Because she is not hungry," said a soldier. "Because she is a mother," said the Sergeant.

VICTOR HUGO

Transformation

Mighty is the force of motherhood! It transforms all things by its vital heat; it turns timidity into fierce courage, and dreadless defiance into tremulous submission; it turns thoughtlessness into foresight, and yet stills all anxiety into calm content; it makes selfishness become self-denial, and gives even to hard vanity the glance of admiring love.

GEORGE ELIOT

Recognition

"I don't want to hear another word!"
I hear my daughter scold.
"Dear me!" I think, "She's awfully strict
For a playful three-year-old!"
She rolls her big eyes heavenward
And sighs with great disdain.
"What am I going to do with you?!"
Her dolls hear her complain.
"Sit down! Be still! Hold out your hands!
Do you have to walk so slow?
Pick up your toys! Go brush your teeth!
Eat all your carrots! Blow!"
I start to tell her how gentle
A mother ought to be
When blushingly, I realize
She's imitating ME!

BARBARA BURROW

My Trust

A picture memory brings to me:
I look across the years and see
Myself beside my mother's knee.

I feel her gentle hand restrain
My selfish moods, and know again
A child's blind sense of wrong and pain.

But wiser now, a man gray grown,
My childhood's needs are better known,
My mother's chastening love I own.

JOHN GREENLEAF WHITTIER

36

A Mother's Love

A mother's love! What can compare with it! Of all things on earth, it comes nearest to divine love in heaven.

A mother's love means a life's devotion—and sometimes a life's sacrifice—with but one thought, one hope and one feeling, that her children will grow up healthy and strong, free from evil habits and able to provide for themselves. Her sole wish is that they may do their part like men and women, avoid dangers and pitfalls, and when dark hours come, trust in Providence to give them strength, patience and courage to bear up bravely.

Happy is the mother when her heart's wish is answered, and happy are her sons and daughters when they can feel that they have contributed to her noble purpose, and, in some measure, repaid her unceasing, unwavering love and devotion.

ANONYMOUS

Little Things

Dear God, please give to me
A thankful heart for little things—
For sunshine on my kitchen floor,
For news the postman brings...

Grant me appreciation
Of small joys that are mine—
The children's birthday parties,
My honeysuckle vine;
The clean, fresh smell
Of clothes just washed;
The ivy on my wall
The children's thrilled delight
To wake and find the first snowfall.
For robins in the springtime,
And autumn's crispy weather—
For leaves that crunch;
Friends in for lunch
And laughter shared together.

...I do not ask contentment
That would ambition stay—
But let me love the little things
I find along the way.

HELEN LOWRIE MARSHALL

The Perfect Mother

...Never was a woman more richly mother than this woman, bubbling over with a hundred little songs and scraps of gay nonsense to beguile a child from tears, and filled with wayward moods as she was, yet her hands were swift to tenderness and care and quiet brooding tending when need arose. Never was she a more perfect mother than during the summers on the mountain top when she could give herself freely to her children. She led them here and there in search of beauty, and she taught them to love cliffs and rugged rocks outlined against the sky, and to love also little dells where ferns and moss grow about a pool. Beauty she brought into her house too and filled the rooms with ferns and flowers.

PEARL BUCK

Flowers for Mother

These velvet roses
    fringed with Queen Anne's Lace,
Do they recall my first bouquet to you?
That ragged bunch of wilted dandelions
You treasured and arranged in your best vase?

The broken stems, the accidental weeds
I brought when I was small,
    received the care
Of lavish blooms in later years. It's true
A mother's love is all a flower needs.

GEORGIA SYKES SULLIVAN

Definition

"Mother" — A word that holds the tender spell
Of the dear essential things of earth;
A home, clean sunlit rooms,
    and the good smell
Of bread, a table spread, a glowing hearth.
And love beyond the dream of anyone...
I search for words for her...
    and there are none.

GRACE NOLL CROWELL

There Was a Child Went Forth

The mother at home quietly placing the dishes
   on the suppertable,
The mother with mild words...a wholesome
   odor falling off her person and clothes as she
   walks by,
The family usages, the language, the company,
   the furniture, the yearning and the
   swelling heart,
Affection that will not be gainsay'd, the
   sense of what is real the thought if after
   all it should prove unreal....
Whether that which appears so is so, or is
it all flashes and specks?
Men and women crowding fast in the streets,
   if they are not flashes and specks what
   are they?
The streets themselves and the facades of
   houses, and goods in the windows....

The village on the highland seen from afar
　　at sunset, the river between. . . .
The strata of color'd clouds, the long bar
　　of maroon-tint away solitary by itself. . . .
The horizon's edge, the flying sea-crow, the
　　fragrance of salt marsh. . . .
These became part of that child who went forth
　　every day, and who now goes, and will
　　always go forth every day.

WALT WHITMAN

In All Honor

Every man, for the sake of the great blessed
Mother in Heaven, and for the love of his own
little mother on earth, should handle all woman-
kind gently, and hold them in all honor.

ALFRED, LORD TENNYSON

The Love of a Mother

There is an enduring tenderness in the love of a mother to a son, that transcends all other affections of the heart. It is neither to be chilled by selfishness, nor daunted by danger, nor weakened by worthlessness, nor stifled by ingratitude. She will sacrifice every comfort to his convenience; she will surrender every pleasure to his enjoyment; she will glory in his fame, and exalt in his prosperity; and if adversity overtake him, he will be the dearer to her by misfortune; and if disgrace settle upon his name, she will still love and cherish him; and if all the world beside cast him off, she will be all the world to him.

WASHINGTON IRVING

Defeat

I know the puppy's very new,
And I know that he's lonely too—
But puppy's place is in the shed,
And not with you, deep down in bed.
Tears will not move me—not at all,
Not even though he's soft and small,
And knows you when you come from play;
The shed's his place and there he'll stay,
    because—
Yes, he has lovely soft big paws,
And yes, I love his ears that flop....
Now, mind: not underneath! On top.

BARBARA A. JONES

The House Beautiful

The Crown of the house is Godliness.
The Beauty of the house is Order.
The Glory of the house is Hospitality.
The Blessing of the house is Contentment.

OLD INSCRIPTION

45

Common Things

Even the kitchen cup I measure by
May hold its quota of blue sky,
Its handful of heaven,
As bread holds leaven.
And a silver faucet stem may bring to me,
The hill's white laughter,
The mountain torrent's ecstacy.

ANGELA MORGAN

Home Fire

Ofttimes across the room you come
To press a kiss against my hair,
To hold me for no cause at all,
Save love. At once our small ones there
Come laughing, make a ring-around.
So does devotion strike a spark
That showers into golden light,
Gathering children in its arc.

VIRGINIA MOODY HAGAN

At Day's End

I hold you in my arms before the fire
And tell the fairy tale you love the best,
While winter twilight deepens and the first
White star comes forth to glitter in the west.

So softly do you lie against my heart
I scarcely know if it be child or flower
I cradle, till you stir and draw a breath
Of wonder at the tale. O, blessed hour

That every mother knows when at day's end
She holds her little child, a wistful ache
Commingling with her joy, and dreams a dream
For him and breathes a prayer for his dear sake!

ADELAIDE LOVE

Wee Laddie

Two dimpled hands,
Ten tiny toes,
One rosebud mouth,
One snubby nose.

A pair of bright eyes,
Twin pools of blue,
Sunshine and showers
Reflecting through.

A soft gurgling laugh,
An innocent smile,
A good healthy yell
Once in a while.

I'm lost in the wonder
Of life's greatest joy
As I gaze on the face
Of my wee sleeping boy.

MILLY WALTON

A Prayer for Mother

O Dear Lord, Thou hast known
  A mother's love and tender care:
    And Thou wilt hear,
    While for my own
  Mother most dear
I make this special prayer.

Protect her life, I pray,
  Who gave the gift of life to me;
    And may she know,
    From day to day,
  The deepening glow
Of joy that comes from Thee.

Ah, hold her by the hand,
  As once her hand held mine;
    And though she may
    Not understand
  Life's winding way,
Lead her in peace divine.

I cannot pay my debt
 For all the love that she has given;
  But Thou, love's Lord,
  Wilt not forget
 Her due reward,
Bless her in earth and heaven.

HENRY VAN DYKE

His Mother

Even He that died for us upon the cross, in the last hour, in the unutterable agony of death, was mindful of His mother, as if to teach us that this holy love should be our last worldly thought — the last point of earth from which the soul should take its flight for heaven.

HENRY WADSWORTH LONGFELLOW

Motherhood

Some day, my son, I hope you know
The joy of watching a small boy grow.
A boy whose laughter makes you warm,
Whose antics run quite true to form.
Whose pants have patches on the knees,
Who climbs the tallest of the trees.
A boy who shelters all stray cats,
Who harbors dogs, and disdains hats.
Whose arms steal round your neck at night,
Whose hands are seldom ever white.
Who gives keen purpose to your life,
Who compensates for each day's strife.
All this I wish so you may know
The joy I had in watching you grow.

EMILY CAREY ALLEMAN

Mother to Babe

Fleck of sky you are,
Dropped through branches dark,
　　O my little one, mine!
Promise of the star
Outpour of the lark;
　　Beam and song divine.

See this precious gift,
Steeping in new birth
　　All my being, for sign
Earth to Heaven can lift,
Heaven descend on earth,
　　Both in one be mine!

Life in light you glass
When you peep and coo,
　　You, my little one, mine!
Brooklet chirps to grass,
Daisy looks in dew
　　Up to dear sunshine.

GEORGE MEREDITH

Somewhere the Child

Among the thousands of tiny things growing up all over the land, some of them under my very wing — watched and tended, unwatched and untended, loved, unloved, protected from danger, thrust into temptation — among them somewhere is the child who will write the novel that will stir men's hearts to nobler issues and incite them to better deeds.

There is the child who will paint the greatest picture or carve the greatest statue of the age; another who will deliver his country in an hour of peril; another who will give his life for a great principle; and another, born more of the spirit than of the flesh, who will live continually on the heights of moral being, and dying, draw men after him.

It may be that I shall preserve one of these children to the race. It is a peg big enough on which to hang a hope, for every child born into the world is a new incarnate thought of God, an ever-fresh and radiant possibility.

KATE DOUGLAS WIGGIN

A Lovely Surprise

Life has started all over for me,
The young years of happiness
Have come again in a sweeter form
Than a mother could ever guess.
The love and devotion I gave my child
I thought I could give no other,
But life held a lovely surprise for me —
This year I became a grandmother.

KAY ANDREW

A Kitchen Window

She hears the twitter of the birds
Finding the largess she has spread,
She sees the beauty snow has wrought
Where winter berries flaunt their red.

The lonely cries of circling gulls
Touch minor chords in her own heart;
In lace-clad tree and crystal bush
She feels a magic counterpart.

She likes the snowman's pixie charm
Created by her wee one's hands;
And looks up from her homely tasks
To share the whimsey he commands.

She has a kinship with the earth
Though busy in her own domain,
And comprehends its noble plan
From just a kitchen window pane.

MILLY WALTON

An Angel on Earth

My mother was an angel on earth. She was a minister of blessing to all human beings within her sphere of action. Her heart was the abode of heavenly purity. She had no feelings but of kindness and beneficence, yet her mind was as firm as her temper was mild and gentle. She had known sorrow, but her sorrow was silent. Had she lived to the age of the Patriarchs every day of her life would have been filled with clouds of goodness and of love. She had been fifty years the delight of my father's heart. If there is existence and retribution beyond the grave, my mother is happy. But if virtue alone is happiness below, never was existence upon earth more blessed than hers.

JOHN QUINCY ADAMS

I'd Rather

I'd rather be a mother
Than anyone on earth—
Bringing up a child or two
Of unpretentious birth.

I'd rather tuck a little child
All safe and sound in bed—
Than twine a chain of diamonds
About my foolish head.

I'd rather wash a smudgy face
With round, bright baby eyes—
Than paint the pageantry of fame,
Or walk among the wise.

MEREDITH GRAY

ACKNOWLEDGMENTS

"Motherhood" by Emily Carey Alleman; copyright 1957 by Emily Carey Alleman.

"Her World" by Bess Streeter Aldrich from THE CUTTERS, *Copyright 1926 by D. Appleton and Company. Copyright renewed 1955 by Bess Streeter Aldrich. Used by permission of Appleton-Century, affiliate of Meredith Press.*

"The Perfect Mother" and "Mother's Hands" by Pearl Buck from THE EXILE, *copyright 1936 Reynal & Hitchcock, Inc.*

"A Mother's Picture" by Alice Cary from ALICE CARY'S WORKS, *Houghton Mifflin Company.*

"Definition" by Grace Noll Crowell; from LIGHT OF THE YEARS, *by Grace Noll Crowell; published by Harper and Brothers.*

"The Palace and the Hut" by Kahlil Gibran, from A TREASURY OF KAHLIL GIBRAN, *Copyright 1951 by the Citadel Press.*

"I'd Rather" by Meredith Gray from POEMS TO MOTHER, *reprinted by permission of Bruce Humphries, Publishers, Boston, Mass.*

Designed by Carole Muller.
Set in Linofilm Palatino,
a 20th century typeface resembling a Venetian,
designed by Hermann Zapf of Frankfurt.
Printed on Hallmark Eggshell Book paper.